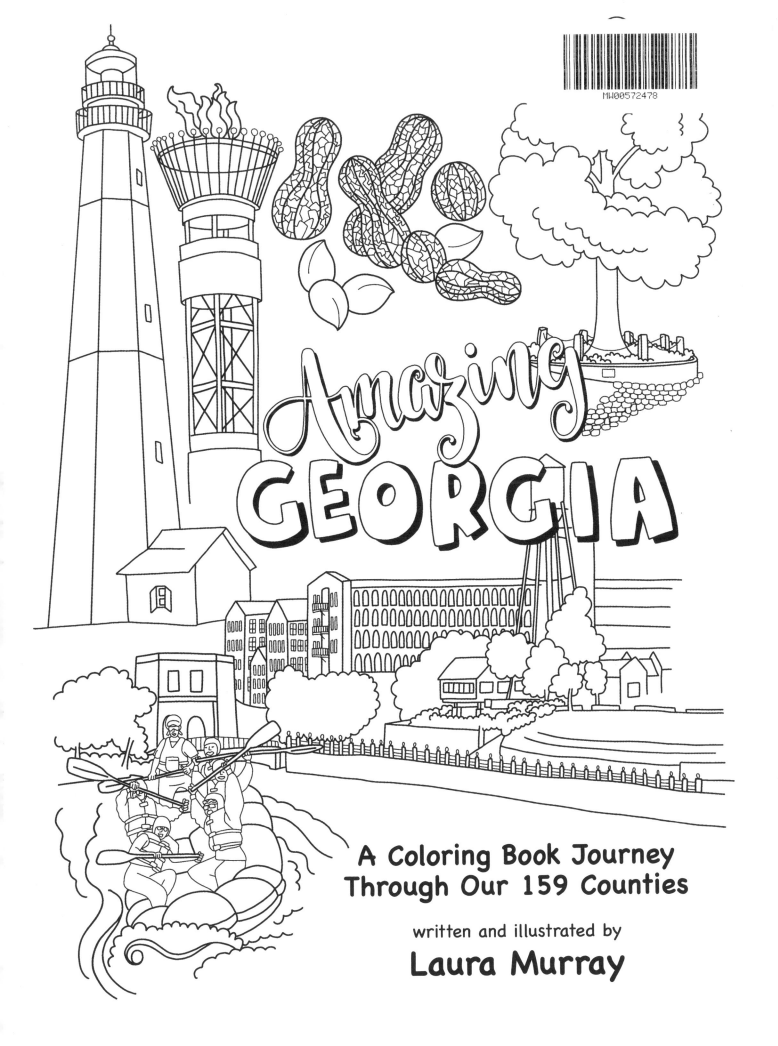

Amazing GEORGIA

A Coloring Book Journey Through Our 159 Counties

written and illustrated by

Laura Murray

NewSouth Books
105 S. Court Street
Montgomery, AL 36104

Cataloging-in-Publication Data

978-1-58838-398-3 (paperback)

Printed in the United States of America by Versa Press

Thank You . . .

I want to thank my wonderful husband Steve for inspiring me with his incredible thirst for knowledge. I want to thank him for holding my hand, for reading everything I wrote, and for catching all those extra commas that I apparently like to throw in everywhere. I would never have become who I am today if he wasn't there motivating me and I'll be forever grateful for his love and encouragement.

For my two Georgia Peaches,

who aren't THAT little anymore.

Mama will always love and support you and

encourage you to follow your dreams.

Amazing Alabama and Amazing Georgia

are proof of mine . . .

USE THIS PAGE TO TEST YOUR MATERIALS

Welcome to our wonderful state—Amazing Georgia.

I have loved coloring for as long as I can remember. Growing up, some of my favorite coloring books had an interesting story, and some just had a fun design. In Amazing Georgia, I have tried to combine a unique design showcasing one or more neat things about all 159 of the counties with a little history thrown in. I begin each county with a good bit of research, but there is no real substitute for hitting the road and exploring Georgia's mountains, big cities, small towns, beaches, farming communities, and country roads in person. All my drawings start with some light pencil sketches before I ink in the details either on paper or on a graphics tablet. Although I love to work in many different types of media, my favorite will always be pen and pencil on paper.

Whether you color north to south, from Dade to Charlton, or hop around on an epic "peach state" road trip, I hope you enjoy this book and are inspired to get out and explore the fun and unique things our state has to offer.

Georgia's 159 Counties

County	#	County	#	County	#	County	#	County	#
Dade	1	Jackson	33	Glascock	65	Candler	96	Long	128
Walker	2	Madison	34	Jefferson	66	Bulloch	97	McIntosh	129
Catoosa	3	Elbert	35	Burke	67	Effingham	98	Clay	130
Whitfield	4	Clarke	36	Troup	68	Stewart	99	Callhoun	131
Murray	5	Oglethorpe	37	Meriwether	69	Webster	100	Dougherty	132
Gilmer	6	Wilkes	38	Pike	70	Schley	101	Tift	133
Fannin	7	Lincoln	39	Lamar	71	Sumter	102	Irwin	134
Union	8	Haralson	40	Monroe	72	Macon	103	Coffee	135
Towns	9	Carroll	41	Jones	73	Dooly	104	Bacon	136
Rabun	10	Douglas	42	Baldwin	74	Pulaski	105	Pierce	137
Chattooga	11	Clayton	43	Washington	75	Dodge	106	Brantley	138
Gordon	12	DeKalb	44	Harris	76	Wheeler	107	Glynn	139
Pickens	13	Rockdale	45	Talbot	77	Montgomery	108	Early	140
Dawson	14	Walton	46	Upson	78	Toombs	109	Miller	141
Lumpkin	15	Oconee	47	Crawford	79	Tattnall	110	Baker	142
White	16	Newton	48	Bibb	80	Evans	111	Mitchell	143
Habersham	17	Morgan	49	Twiggs	81	Bryan	112	Colquitt	144
Stephens	18	Greene	50	Wilkinson	82	Chatham	113	Cook	145
Floyd	19	Taliaferro	51	Johnson	83	Liberty	114	Berrien	146
Bartow	20	Warren	52	Emanuel	84	Quitman	115	Lanier	147
Cherokee	21	McDuffie	53	Jenkins	85	Randolph	116	Atkinson	148
Forsyth	22	Columbia	54	Screven	86	Terrell	117	Clinch	149
Hall	23	Richmond	55	Muscogee	87	Lee	118	Ware	150
Banks	24	Heard	56	Chatta-		Worth	119	Charlton	151
Franklin	25	Coweta	57	hoochee	88	Crisp	120	Camden	152
Hart	26	Fayette	58	Marion	89	Wilcox	121	Seminole	153
Polk	27	Spalding	59	Taylor	90	Turner	122	Decatur	154
Paulding	28	Henry	60	Peach	91	Ben Hill	123	Grady	155
Cobb	29	Butts	61	Houston	92	Telfair	124	Thomas	156
Fulton	30	Jasper	62	Bleckley	93	Jeff Davis	125	Brooks	157
Gwinnett	31	Putnam	63	Laurens	94	Appling	126	Lowndes	158
Barrow	32	Hancock	64	Treutlen	95	Wayne	127	Echols	159

7

From its red-brick Greek Revival courthouse to the ancient Etowah Indian
Mounds, Bartow County, founded in 1832, is full of history, style, and cotton
farming. Cooper's Iron Works was an early furnace and foundry owned by
Mark Anthony Cooper, who built an entire town, named Etowah, to support the
iron works. Most of the complex was destroyed by Sherman's army during the
Civil War. Young Brothers Pharmacy in Cartersville sports the world's very first
Coca-Cola mural, dating back to 1894.

Carroll

Carroll County, formed in 1826, is home to the second major gold rush in the United States. McIntosh Reserve Park offers hiking and outdoor recreation for the whole family. It contains part of Creek Chief William McIntosh's plantation and a reconstructed version of his log cabin. The Platanthera integrilabia (white fringeless orchid) calls Carroll County home but is now on the threatened species list. Historic Banning Mills is an outdoor adventure park with ziplines, nature trails, treehouse overnight camping, and more.

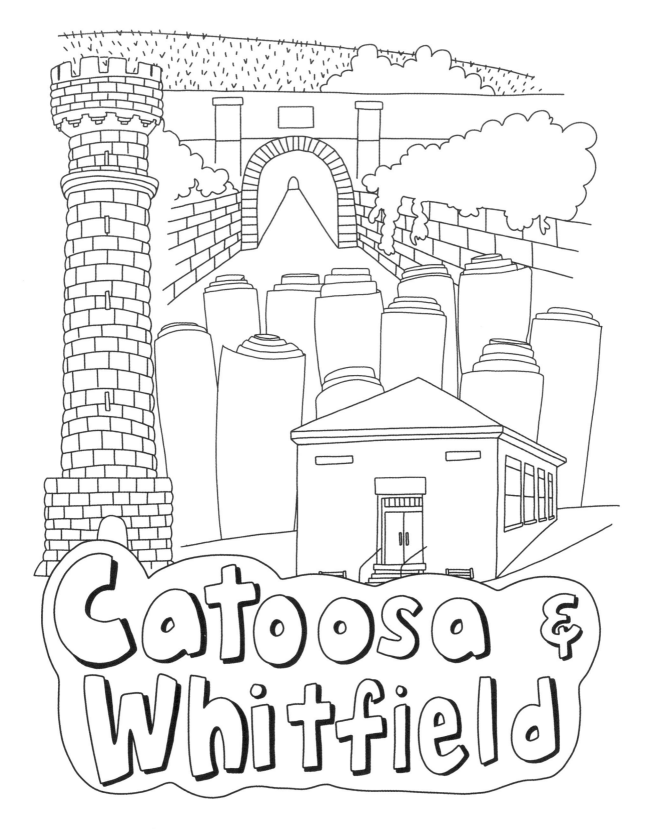

Catoosa & Whitfield

Catoosa County, formed in 1851, is home to the Stone Church, built from rocks found in the surrounding countryside, and Chickamauga, a Civil War battlefield. At Chickamauga, a spiral staircase leads to the top of Wilder Tower, from which most of the battlefield can be seen. In Whitfield County, Tunnel Hill is home to an almost 1,500-foot tunnel that cuts through Chetoogeta Mountain. Established in 1851, Whitfield County is also home to the town of Dalton, known as the "Carpet Capital of the World" because more than 150 carpet manufacturers operate in the area.

The Chieftains Museum is a two-story dogtrot log cabin that was once the home of Cherokee leader Major Ridge and his family. Today it is an interpretive museum showcasing the culture and history of the Cherokee people. The Clock Tower in Rome is one of the oldest landmarks in the city. Founded in 1832, Floyd County is home to Berry College, a four-year Christian liberal arts college. In 2012, two bald eagles began nesting in the tall pines around campus. Today, people from all over the world watch the eagles through live video feeds of the nests.

Murray

Murray County, established in 1832, has one of the two   Palladian-style courthouses in the state. Another important piece of Georgia history in Murray County is the Chief Vann House. Chief Vann was a Native American leader, and his home was the largest and most affluent plantation in the Cherokee Nation. In this mountainous area of North Georgia, the Percina kusha (bridled darter) makes its home in the rivers and streams. On top of Fort Mountain, a mysterious rock wall remains as evidence of the ancient people who once called this region home.

Walker & Dade

Walker County, founded in 1833, is home to the Chattooga Academy, which was the site of the Battle of LaFayette during the American Civil War. A beautiful but threatened species of herb, Marshallia mohrii (Mohr's Barbara buttons), grows in this part of northwest Georgia. The historic Dade County courthouse, built in 1926, was designed in the Dutch colonial revival style. Established in 1837, Dade County is also home to Rock City, where the breathtaking view at Lover's Leap has been an iconic Lookout Mountain destination for generations of travelers.

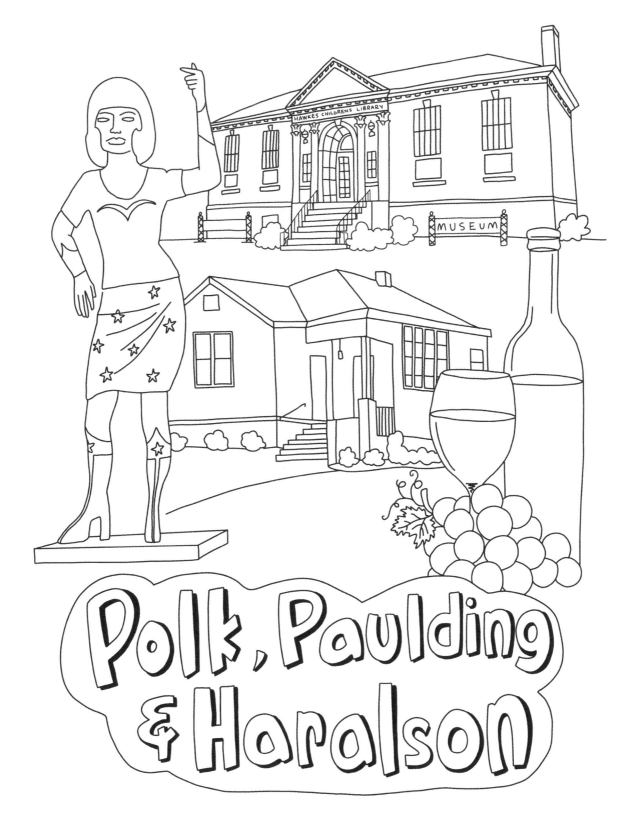

Polk, Paulding & Haralson

Polk County was created in 1851. The county historical society owns Hawkes Children's Library in Cedartown. At eighteen feet tall, the Uniroyal Gal in Paulding County is a larger-than-life roadside attraction. Established in 1832, Paulding County is also home to the historic Hiram Colored School, which was the only Rosenwald School in Paulding County. It is now a museum which shares the history of African American education during segregation. Haralson County was founded in 1856, and the town of Budapest has a rich history of Hungarian farmers who settled the town and grew abundant vineyards.

Chattooga & Gordon

One of the world's largest denim plants, Mount Vernon Mills, is located in Chattooga County. Founded in 1838, Chattooga County is also home to the historic Sardis Baptist Church, which is actually older than the county itself. Gordon County was created in 1850 and is home to New Echota, a state historic site that celebrates the Cherokee people who once called this area home. The first Native American newspaper, the Cherokee Phoenix, was published here in 1828. Also in Gordon County is Paradise Gardens, a unique folk-art park created by the Reverend Howard Finster.

Cherokee & Pickens

The Rock Barn in Cherokee County was built in 1906 with rocks from the Etowah River. Established in 1832, Cherokee County also has a long history of poultry and dairy farming. Pickens County was created in 1853 and is home to the Georgia Marble Festival, where thousands gather each year for arts and crafts, a 5k fun run, a parade, and sculpting demonstrations. The old Pickens County jail in Jasper was constructed with local marble. The jailer and his family lived on the first floor while the prisoners' cell blocks were upstairs.

In Gilmer County, established in 1832, the historic Cartecay Methodist Church is made of hand-hewn virgin pine. Also in Gilmer County is the beloved Poole's BBQ, with its famous "Pig Hill Of Fame." With several orchards to choose from, Fannin County's most famous crop is its crisp and juicy apples. Established in 1854, Fannin County is home to the Blue Ridge Scenic Railway, a 26-mile round trip through the picturesque North Georgia mountains.

Towns
Union
Rabun
Habersham
Lumpkin
White
Stephens
Franklin
Dawson
Hall
Banks
Hart
Forsyth
Jackson
Elbert
Madison
Barrow

Northeast
Georgia
Mountains

One of the largest reservoirs in Georgia, Lake Lanier attracts millions of tourists each year. Founded in 1818, Hall County is now known as the "poultry capital of the world," with several poultry-processing plants in the area. Brenau University is a private liberal arts school with a gorgeous historic campus in Gainesville. Also in Gainesville is a twenty-foot rabbit statue, which is a memorial to the town's previous name—Rabbittown. In the hills of Hall County lies a vein of clay, which has been mined and sculpted into crocks, face jugs, and other clay creations for over 150 years by the artists in Gillsville.

Credited with the first use of ether as surgical anesthesia, Crawford Long was a notable resident of Jackson County. Established in 1796, Jackson County is home to Georgia's oldest registered Angus cow herd and today ranks in the top ten for cattle production in the state. The Pendergrass Flea Market, the largest indoor flea market in the U.S., has over 25,000 visitors each weekend. The beautiful courthouse in Jackson was constructed in 1879 and is notable as being one of the first courthouses built in Georgia after the Civil War.

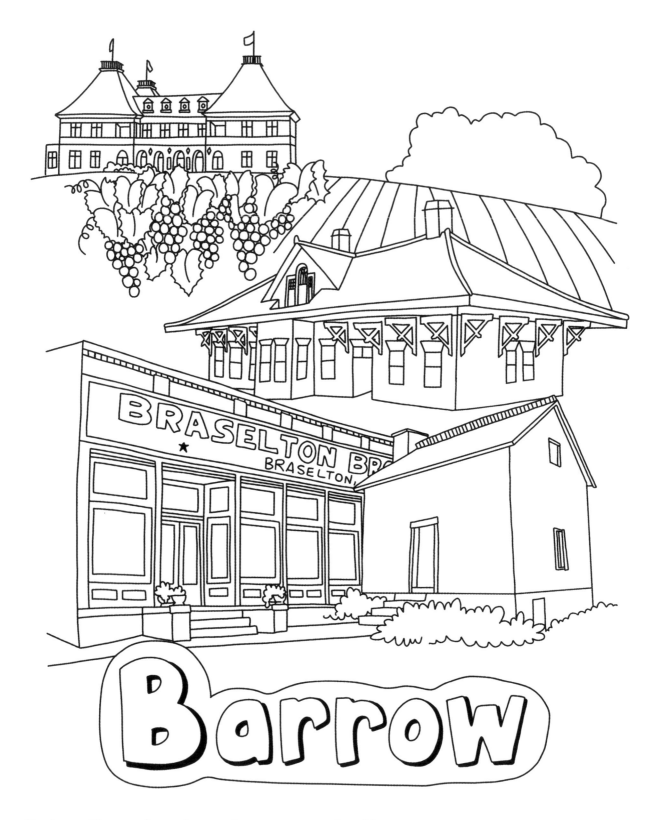

Barrow

Chateau Elan, a luxurious winery, spa and golf resort, calls Barrow County home. Founded in 1914, Barrow County is also home to the Braselton Brothers Department Store, which was built in 1904 and provided one-stop shopping for the modern family. It included a mercantile, a supermarket, appliance sales, a post office, a bank, a newspaper, and a railroad office under the same roof. The Winder Depot was constructed for the Seabord Air Line Railroad in 1910 and now houses the local chamber of commerce. Fort Yargo State Park is built around a 1792 frontier cabin and offers a wide array of outdoor recreation.

Rabun County was created in 1819. The York House Inn, founded in 1896, is the state's oldest continuously operating bed-and-breakfast. Tallulah Gorge is one of Georgia's popular outdoor destinations and has a suspension bridge high in the sky. Foxfire started as a series of books in the 1960s to help preserve the traditions of the people in the Appalachian mountains. Goats on the Roof, a tourist stop in Tiger, is just as funny as it sounds. The over sixty-year-old Clayton Cafe is one of the most popular restaurants in the area. Psilocybe weilii is a type of wild mushroom that only grows in the Rabun County area.

Welcome
GEORGIA MOUNTAIN FAIR
The show Place of the Mountain

WORLDS LARGEST AMISH CHAIR

Union & Towns

Union County, created in 1832, is the home of Brasstown Bald, Georgia's tallest mountain. The visitor center on top provides a 360-degree view of Georgia, South Carolina, North Carolina, and Tennessee. Another attraction you can't miss is the "World's Largest Amish Chair" in Blairsville. Established in 1856, Towns County has many mountain attractions for the whole family. Thousands of visitors flock to Hiawassee each July for the Georgia Mountain Fair. Hamilton Gardens features the largest collection of rhododendrons in the Southeast, with over 1,500 rhododendrons and native azaleas.

Pierce Memorial Hall, in Dahlonega, is the oldest building on the University of North Georgia's campus. The gold steeple, added in the 1970s, is made of genuine Dahlonega gold. Lumpkin County, established in 1832, is home to the nation's first gold rush in 1828. Also in Dahlonega is the beautifully restored 1948 Holly Theater. Dawson County was created in 1857, and is where tourists come from all around to view Amicalola Falls, the highest waterfall in Georgia. Forsyth County, also founded in 1832, is where you can see two gigantic Pink Panther statues which are a must-see photo-op in the town of Cumming.

The Big Red Apple monument in Cornelia is dedicated to the apple harvest, once an important part of the county's economy. Habersham County, formed in 1818, is home to the Chenocetah Fire Tower, built during the Great Depression and open one day each year. In 1857, White County was created. You can visit Babyland General Hospital in Cleveland to see Cabbage Patch dolls being born. Helen, in White County, is where Nora Mill Granary has been grinding grains since 1876. The Nacoochee Mound, on the banks of the Chattahoochee River, is a traditional Mississippian burial ground, but is not open to the public.

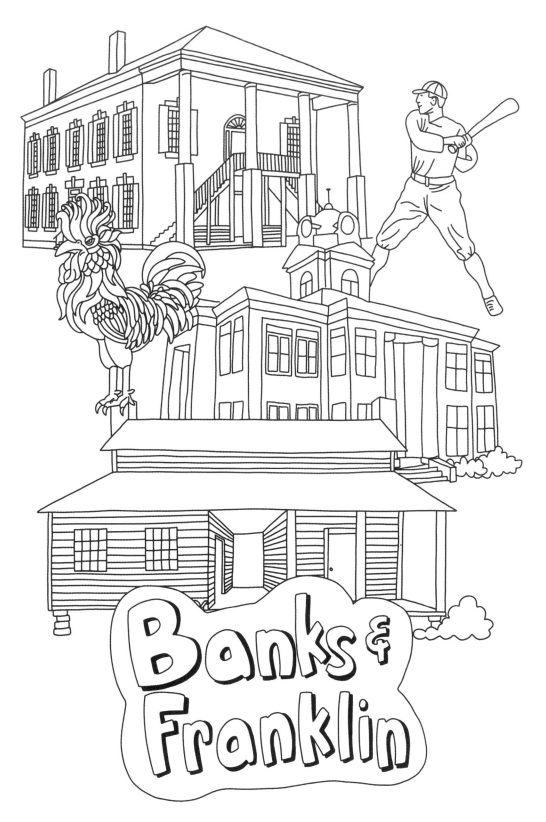

Banks & Franklin

Franklin County was established in 1784 and was the first county created in Georgia after the Revolutionary War. The county courthouse in Carnesville is a beautiful example of neoclassical architecture. A famous resident of Franklin County, baseball Hall of Famer Ty Cobb, is celebrated at the Ty Cobb Museum in Royston. Construction on the Banks County Courthouse began in 1860, just 2 years after the county was founded. Banks County is home to Fort Hollingsworth, an early frontier fort built in the late 1700s. Today, a bustling poultry business is important to the local economy.

Stephens & Hart

Stephens County, established in 1905, is known for its scenic beauty. At 186 feet tall, Toccoa Falls is a breathtaking landmark at Toccoa Falls College. Traveler's Rest, a state historic site, provides a glimpse into northeast Georgia mountain life in the 1800s. Lake Hartwell is a man-made reservoir between Georgia and South Carolina and is one of the Southeast's most popular lakes. Hart County, founded in 1853, has a wonderful community theater in a restored railroad warehouse in Hartwell. Quilt squares displayed on the sides of buildings and around Hartwell reflect the rich local history of quilting.

Madison
& Elbert

Elbert County, known as the "Granite Capital of the World," was established in 1790 and has a vibrant historical society headquartered in the restored train depot. Called "America's Stonehenge," the Georgia Guidestones are massive stone panels which function as an astronomical calendar. Danielsville Hardware in Madison County is an eclectic roadside store in the county seat. Formed in 1811, Madison County is also home to Watson Mill Bridge State Park. This picturesque park includes Georgia's longest wooden bridge still in use and lots of opportunities for outdoor activities.

Douglas
Cobb
Gwinnett
DeKalb
Fulton
Clayton
Coweta
Fayette

Atlanta Metro

The Root House Museum is the oldest house in Marietta—county seat of Cobb County—and is used to educate us about life during the mid-1800s. Founded in 1832, Cobb is also home to The General, a locomotive made famous during the Great Locomotive Chase of 1862, which is housed at the Southern Museum of Civil War & Locomotive History. Kennesaw Mountain National Battlefield Park preserves the history of a key battle during the Atlanta Campaign. Another icon in Cobb County is the Big Chicken, a 56-foot chicken on top of a KFC. Six Flags Over Georgia is home to the Riverview Carousel, built in 1908.

Established in 1853, Fulton County is home to the State Capitol. Our 39th president's official archives are housed at the Jimmy Carter Presidential Library and Museum. The Atlanta History Center is a museum and historical research center in the Buckhead district. People often pose with the statue of Willy B at Zoo Atlanta in Grant Park. Close by is Ebenezer Baptist Church, where Martin Luther King Jr. preached. Atlanta's Georgia Tech is an engineering-focused university. The Varsity is the world's largest drive-in, and the beautiful Fox Theater is a performing arts venue that opened in 1929.

Douglas

Visit the ruins of the Civil War-era mill at Sweetwater Creek State Park in Lithia Springs for outdoor activities such as canoeing, hiking, camping, picnicking, and fishing. While you're there, look for the threatened Gratiola amphiantha (snorkelwort), which grows in the shallow pools along the bank. Founded in 1870, Douglas County has one of the more unusual courthouses in the state. Built in the International Style, it is now home to the Douglas County Museum of History and Art. One odd roadside photo-op in Douglasville is a larger-than-life 15-foot tall mailbox.

In 1818, when Gwinnett County was founded, much of the planning for the new county took place in the historic Elisha Wynn house, which is now open for tours. The Lawrenceville Female Seminary was originally built in the 1830s, but today it houses the Gwinnett History Museum. The population of Gwinnett County has outgrown the old historic courthouse. Today the building is used as a venue for weddings, concerts, and other special events. The Little Mulberry Indian Mounds are a series of 200 stone piles created by the Native Americans who formerly lived in the area.

DeKalb County is home to the Centers for Disease Control and Prevention, the federal agency responsible for the nation's health security. Emory University, established in 1836, is almost as old as the county itself, which was founded in 1822. The Glenn Memorial Methodist Church is a historic building on campus that is also used as an auditorium. DeKalb County is home to both Waffle and Huddle House, 24-hour diners that serve up a mean breakfast, lunch, dinner, or midnight snack. Seen from miles around, Stone Mountain is situated in Stone Mountain Park and has camping and attractions for the whole family.

Built in 1840, the historic Warren House—now a special event venue—
saw intense fighting in the Civil War. The Pulitzer-Prize winning novel Gone
with the Wind, about the spoiled daughter of a Civil War planter, was set in
Clayton County and Atlanta. Clayton County, which was founded in 1858, is
also home to Hartsfield-Jackson Atlanta International Airport, the busiest in
the world. Its almost 400-feet high control tower is the tallest in the United
States. A cultural landmark in Jonesboro is the Atlanta State Farmers Market,
the largest outdoor farmers market of its kind in the United States.

With more than 100 miles of cart-legal trails and paths, Peachtree City is called the "golf cart capital of the world." Fayette County was established in 1821. Its antebellum Holliday Dorsey Fife house, in the middle of downtown Fayetteville, is a historic museum open for tours. Built in 1825, the old county courthouse has the longest courthouse bench in the world. The historic Starr's Mill, a popular place to fish and take photographs, is only about 25 miles south of Atlanta.

Coweta

The W. A. Brannon Mercantile and Moreland Knitting Mill is now home to the Moreland Welcome Center and museum. Established in 1825, Coweta County was the home of famed author and comedian Lewis Grizzard, who has a special menu item named for him at Sprayberry's BBQ--a barbecue sandwich served with Brunswick stew and onion rings. With the original stained glass, slate roof, and beautiful Victorian-style woodwork, the Parrott Camp Soucy House in Newnan is now a bed-and-breakfast. The historic Coweta County courthouse is a Classical Revival style with a beautiful copper dome.

Clarke

Rockdale

Walton

Oconee

Newton

Morgan

Henry

Jasper

Putnam

Butts

Lamar

Baldwin

monroe

Jones

Wilkinson

Bibb

Crawford

Twiggs

Peach

Houston

Historic Heartland

Created in 1801, Clarke County is home to several unique attractions. The Tree That Owns Itself is on a cobblestone street and has a fund set aside for its perpetual care. The nation's only double-barrel cannon (never fired) is located at City Hall. The Morton Building housed African American professional offices and a theater for much of its history. The Georgia Theater is an iconic live music venue in downtown Athens. The University of Georgia's arches welcome visitors to the first state-chartered university in the United States. The Taylor Grady House is a historic home that is open for tours and as an event space.

Robins Air Force Base in Warner Robins is a major military base focused on logistics. Founded in 1821, Houston County is also home to the Georgia National Fair, a state-sponsored fair that is held every October. The beautiful Perry United Methodist Church was organized in 1826, but the church building dates to the 1860s. The Go Fish Education Center offers an educational journey through Georgia's watersheds and helps teach the public about wildlife, habitats, and the impact of water pollution on the environment.

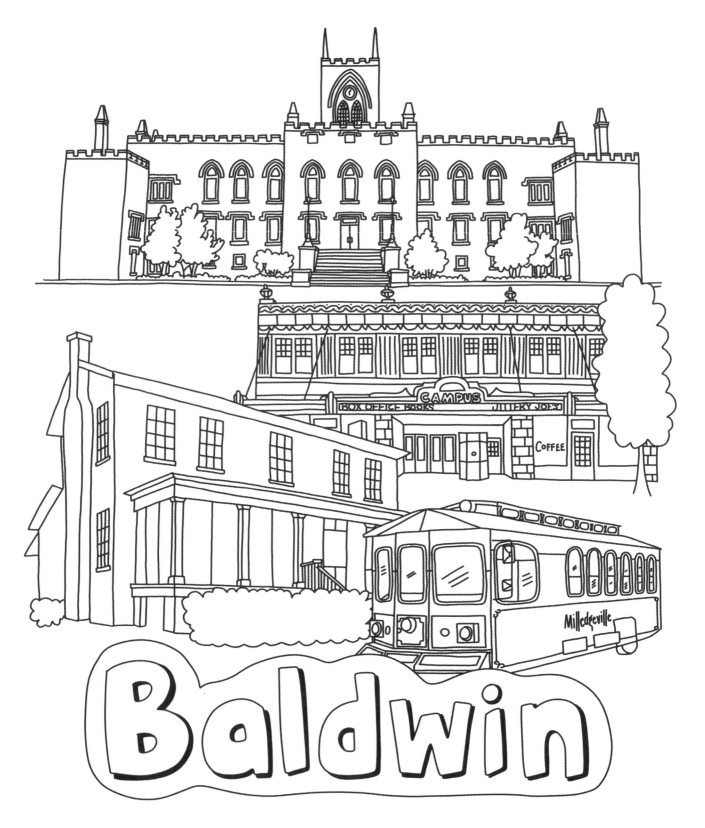

Baldwin County and its county seat, Milledgeville, played an important part in Georgia's history. Founded in 1903, the county was the home of the state's first "frontier" capital. The Old State Capitol building is now a museum. Andalusia, home of Flannery O'Connor, was first built in the mid-1800s as a working plantation. The Campus Theater is a beautifully restored art deco theater in downtown Milledgeville. While in Milledgeville, be sure to take a guided trolley tour through the picturesque streets of the historic downtown.

Bibb

Fort Hawkins was established in 1806 on the bank of the Ocmulgee River at the border of the Creek Nation. The community that grew around the fort would become the town of Macon. Close by, the Ocmulgee National Monument is evidence of the thriving Native American culture that was here 1000 years ago. Macon's first church, Christ Church Episcopal, is a Gothic-style building with beautiful stained-glass windows. The Hay House is a historic home built in the 1850s and is open for tours. Nu-Way Weiners opened in 1916 and is one of the oldest hotdog restaurants in the United States.

Henry

Henry County was founded in 1821 with McDonough   as the county seat.
Shingleroof is among the oldest active Methodist campgrounds in the state
with meetings date back to the 1830s. The extravagant train depot in Hampton
was the county's only rail connection from the 1840s to 1882 and included a
cotton warehouse in the same building as the passenger area. Today Henry
County is the home of the Atlanta Motor Speedway, a world-class NASCAR
1.5-mile oval race track and event venue. Noah's Ark Animal Sanctuary is a
250-acre sanctuary for abused animals.

In Remembrance

Walton & Rockdale

Built in 1883, the Walton County Courthouse is one of two identical courthouses in Georgia. One famous resident of Walton County was Moina Belle Michael, who initiated the sale of paper poppies to raise money for wounded WWI soldiers. Founded in 1870, Rockdale County is home to the Blue Willow Inn—one of the South's restaurants with all-you-can-eat Southern cooking. Originally built for the 1996 Olympics, the Georgia International Horse Park in Conyers is a premier equestrian facility. The Monastery of the Holy Spirit is home to monks dedicated to a life of silence, work, and prayer.

Oconee & Morgan

Built in the late 1790s, the Eagle Tavern is one of the oldest structures in Oconee County and is open for tours. Just outside Watkinsville is a unique piece of artwork known as the Iron Horse. Classic City Clydesdales, a world-class Clydesdale breeding facility, is located in Oconee County, which was founded in 1875. Located in downtown Madison, Heritage Hall is a historic house museum with period furnishings. Morgan County, established in 1807, is home to the Madison Morgan Cultural Center, a program located in the 1890s school building. They offer education in visual arts, dance, music, and history.

Newton & Butts

The Brick Store, the oldest brick structure in Newton County, was built in 1821 and has been a general store, stagecoach stop, post office, jail, and residence in its years. Newton County was established in 1831, and the historic Newton County courthouse is still being used today. Founded in 1825, Butts County is home to some of the most beautiful flora in the area. Visit the Dauset Trails Nature Center near Jackson to view the abundance of azaleas native to this part of Georgia. The Indian Springs Hotel in Butts County, built in 1825, has been restored and converted into a museum.

Jasper & Putnam

Created in 1807, Jasper County is named for a Revolutionary War hero who died during the Siege of Savannah. A beautiful 1820s home, Reese Hall is now a bed and breakfast. The Bank of Shadydale is all that remains of a thriving row of storefronts. In its history, the bank also served as a post office, city hall, and a library. Putnam County, also founded in 1807, has a Carnegie Library, still in use today. The Dairy Festival held each year in Eatonton, celebrates the dairy industry's importance. Rock Eagle, a stone effigy mound on the grounds of a 4H camp, was built 2000 years ago by Native Americans.

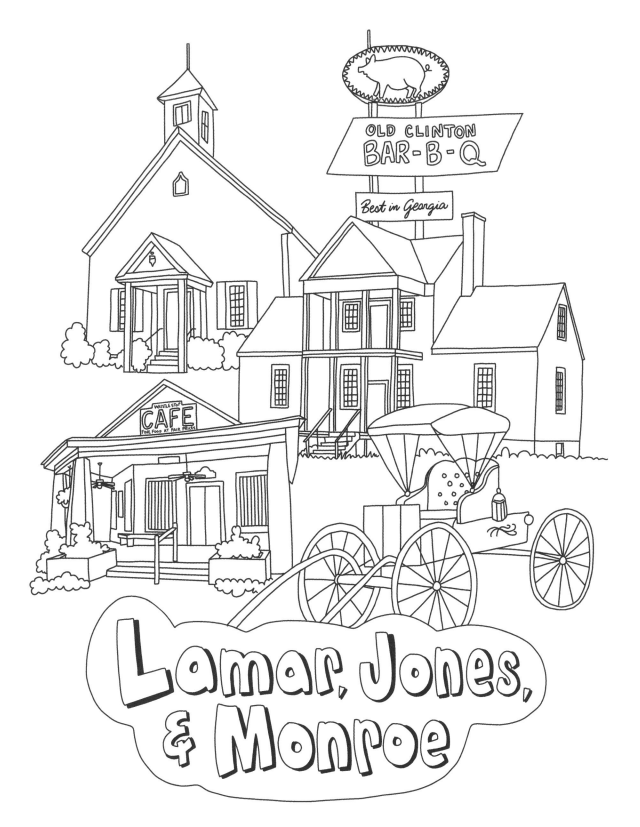

Lamar, Jones, & Monroe

Lamar County was created in 1920 and is famous for the Barnesville Buggy Days Festival, which celebrates the "Buggy Capital of the South." Monroe County, established in 1821, is home to the Whistle Stop Cafe, which was opened after the movie Fried Green Tomatoes made the town of Juliette famous. Jones County, founded in 1807, is home to the Clinton United Methodist Church. The active church was built around 1921. The Old Clinton Bar-B-Q in Grey has been called the "best in Georgia" since 1958. Also in Jones County is the Cabaniss-Hanberry House, which was built in 1805.

Crawford & Peach

The Blue Bird Corporation put Fort Valley on the map with its schoolbus headquarters and manufacturing facility. Located in Peach County, which was founded in 1824, Fort Valley is also known as the Peach Capital of Georgia for the number of peaches grown in the area. The Austin Theater in downtown Fort Valley has been beautifully restored to its original glory. Created in 1822, Crawford County has one of the most picturesque courthouses in the state. It was the oldest courthouse still in use in Georgia until a new one was built in 2001.

Twiggs & Wilkinson

Founded in 1908, Twiggs County is known as the geographic center of Georgia. People have been worshiping at the historic Richland Baptist Church in Twiggs County for over 200 years. Wilkinson County was established in 1903, and its major economic exports include soybeans, corn, and peanuts. Deposits of kaolin, a type of clay used in medicines, is mined near Gordon.

Oglethorpe

Lincoln

Taliaferro

Columbia

Wilkes

McDuffie

Greene

Richmond

Warren

Hancock

Jefferson

Burke

Glascock

Washington

Emanuel

Jenkins

Johnson

Classic South

Columbia

Columbia County, established in 1790, is home to Heggie's Rock, a dome-shaped granite outcrop with shallow pools of water where rare plants grow. The county courthouse in Appling was built in 1812 and is the oldest one in Georgia still in use. The water tower in Harlem bears the face of comedian Oliver Hardy, who was born there. The picturesque Kiokee Baptist Church in Appling was originally formed in 1772, and the building is still in use today.

Richmond

Richmond County, created in 1777, is one of Georgia's original counties. The Augusta Cotton Exchange Building was built in the mid 1880s at the height of the cotton trade. The Gertrude Herbert Institute of Art, in the Ware-Sibley-Clark House, is an independent art school and offers classes and gallery space. Spanning the Augusta Canal, the Butt Memorial Bridge, built in 1914, was the first memorial to a victim of the Titanic disaster. Opened in 1933, the Augusta National Golf Club is one of the most famous in the world. Since 1934, they have hosted The Masters, one of the nation's major golf tournaments.

Burke & Jenkins

Burke County, established in 1732, is one of Georgia's eight original counties. The courthouse was built in 1857 and is one of the oldest in the state still in use. The bird dog cemetery at Di-Lane Plantation preserves the South's sporting past with over 75 headstones dedicated to the pure-bred bird dogs that are buried there. Some of the major economic crops in Jenkins County are wheat, soybeans, corn and peanuts. The Big Buckhead Baptist Church is located in Jenkins County, which was founded in 1905. The church was built in 1845, but the congregation dates to before the Revolutionary War.

Johnson & Emanuel

Founded in 1858, Johnson County is home to the John B. Wright house, one of the oldest homes in south Georgia. The Grice Inn in Wrightsville has a unique style and was originally constructed as a home and hotel in 1905. The town of Stilmore has a larger-than-life rooster sculpture dedicated to the poultry industry, prevalent in the local economy. The George L. Smith State Park in Emanuel County, established in 1812, offers serene outdoor adventure amongst the cypress filled waters of Twin City.

The Mitchell Depot Historical Museum is located in the old train depot in Glascock County, founded in 1857. In Warren County, established in 1793, the restored Knox Theatre has been home to many different kinds of shows, vaudeville acts, and musical performances over the years. Hickory Hill is a historic house museum in Thomson and is open for tours. Thomson is located in McDuffie County, which was created in 1870, and is home to the Rock House, the oldest stone residence in Georgia.

ON THIS SPOT
IN 1933
DURING THE GREAT DEPRESSION
NEIGHBORS OF A FARMER NAMED
BARTOW BARRON
JOINED TOGETHER TO RESCUE HIS PIG
FROM A DRY WELL

Washington & Jefferson

Washington County, Georgia's 10th, was formed in 1784. One of the oldest jails in the state, reportedly built to hold Vice President Aaron Burr while on his way to trial for treason, is in Warthen. The restored Brown House in Sandersville is a museum owned by the Washington County Historical Society. In Jefferson County, established in 1796, the Market House is a reminder of the slave trade that once existed throughout the South. One of the most endearing roadside monuments in Jefferson County is in memory of a group of friends who banded together to help a neighbor get his pig out of a well.

Created in 1793, Hancock County was named for John Hancock, signer of the Declaration of Independence. The congregation of the Powelton Baptist Church dates back to 1786, and its building hosted the creation of the Georgia Baptist Convention in 1822. The picturesque Baxter's/Millmore Mill is a grist mill built around 1800 on Shoulderbone Creek. Green County was established in 1796, and the courthouse in Greensboro originally had a Masonic Lodge on the third floor. The Old Gaol (jail) was built in 1807 with walls two feet thick and made of local granite.

Oglethorpe & Taliaferro

Taliaferro County, founded in 1825, is where you can visit A. H. Stephens State Park. The park features a historic home, Liberty Hall, and one of Georgia's largest collections of Civil War artifacts. In Oglethorpe County, established in 1793, county government operates in a beautiful 1887 courthouse. The Beth-Salem Presbyterian Church in Lexington is one of Georgia's most historic rural churches, dating back to 1785. Shaking Rock, a unique natural rock formation in Lexington, is a 27-ton boulder that was so finely balanced on the rock beneath it that the boulder could be shaken by the force of your hand.

Wilkes County, created in 1777, was Georgia's first county. The Mary Willis Library in Washington was built in 1889. Visit the Callaway Plantation for a glimpse into life before modern conveniences. The Grey House, built around 1790, was never modernized with indoor plumbing or electricity. In Lincoln County, founded in 1796, the Chennault House is known for a raid on the property during the Civil War. Approximately $250,000, part of the Confederate treasury, was stolen back from Union troops. A great example of a rural schoolhouse, the Amity School is used today as a community center.

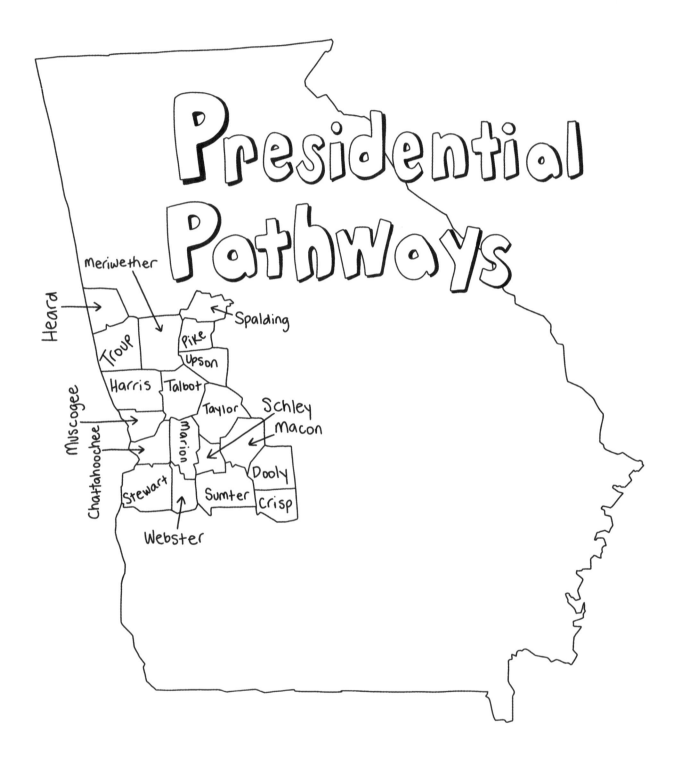

Presidential Pathways

Meriwether

Heard

Spalding

Troup

Pike

Upson

Harris

Talbot

Taylor

Schley

Macon

Muscogee

Marion

Chattahoochee

Dooly

Stewart

Sumter

Crisp

Webster

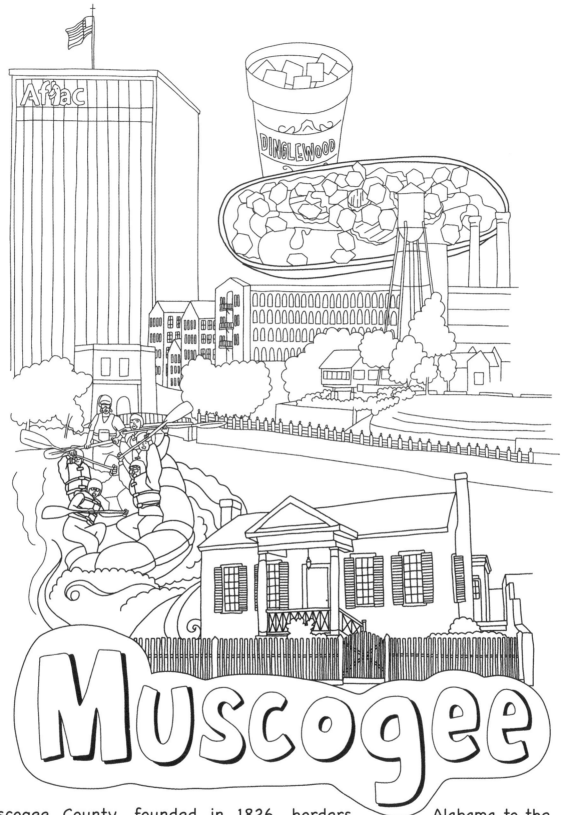

Muscogee

Muscogee County, founded in 1826, borders Alabama to the west. The Riverwalk is a 15-mile long park on the banks of the Chattahoochee and in the shadow of historic textile mills. The river offers the world's longest urban whitewater course where you can kayak, raft, or zip-line. The tallest building in the county is home to Aflac. Founded in 1955, Aflac now operates internationally. Dr. Pemberton lived in Columbus in the 1850s and developed the original formula for Coca-Cola. Dinglewood Pharmacy continues its 100 year history of serving "scrambled dogs" to generations of Columbus families.

Spalding

The University of Georgia-affiliated Georgia Experiment Station in Griffin is a premier agricultural research facility and has played an important role in the development of modern Southern agriculture since 1888. Established in 1851, Spalding County is home to the Old Gassiert Homeplace, built in 1827. The famous gunfighter John Henry "Doc" Holliday was born in Griffin in 1851 and lived in Georgia until he moved out west for his health.

Troup County, created in 1825, has an unusual Stripped Classical style courthouse built during the 1930s as part of the New Deal. Charlie Joseph's in downtown, boasts the "world's best hotdog" and has been in business since 1920. The Azalea Storytelling Festival in LaGrange celebrates the art of storytelling with a weekend-long event every spring, and is recognized as one of the oldest festivals of its kind in Georgia. In 2009, a new manufacturing plant for Kia automobiles began rolling new cars off the assembly line in West Point, and with it over 15,000 new jobs were created.

Heard & Meriwether

Meriwether County, founded in 1827, is known for Warm Springs—where Franklin D. Roosevelt loved to vacation because of the healing spring water. His home, the Little White House, is open for tours and showcases several of the president's personal items and cars. The President Theatre in Manchester is an art-deco masterpiece built in 1935. The antebellum Greenville Presbyterian Church was built in 1836. Forestry is the mainstay of the economy in Heard County, established in 1830. The Heard County Historical Center and Museum, located in Franklin's old jail, is open on Tuesday and Thursday.

Pike County, established in 1822, is home to the Peach State Aerodrome, a public/private airport modeled after the original Atlanta airport. The airport has a museum and a youth aviation program where students learn to restore and fly airplanes. The Ritz Theatre in Upson County, forced in 1824, was built in 1927 and is still open seven days a week. The county courthouse in Thomaston was built in 1908. Also in Thomaston is the Piggie Park BBQ, a 1950s style drive-in with the best BBQ in the area. Upson County is also home to Skydive Atlanta, where you can learn to conquer the skies

Harris County, established in 1827, is home to the plumleaf azalea, possibly the rarest in the eastern United States. Franklin D. Roosevelt's favorite picnic spot is memorialized with a bronze statue on top of Pine Mountain. The Hamilton Baptist Church is a unique Victorian design from 1890. Talbot County was also formed in 1827 and was formerly home to LeVert College, a Methodist school for women. The Straus family founded the school and went on to establish Macy's department store. Zion Episcopal Church in Talbotton is a beautiful example of a church built in the English Tudor and carpenter-gothic style.

Chattahoochee, Marion & Schley

Fort Benning, home of the U.S. Army Infantry, covers nearly 170,000 acres in Chattahoochee County. The "jump towers" built for the 1939 World's Fair are now used for paratrooper training. The two-story Old Cusseta Jail was built in 1902. Chattahoochee County, established in 1854, is home to Pasaquan, a seven-acre folk art compound created by visionary artist Eddie Martin. Marion County, home to the Old Marion County Courthouse, was created in 1827. The Schley County Courthouse has a beautiful clock tower. Formed in 1857, Schley County sees raising poultry and cattle as being the base of their economy.

IDEAL
HE ONLY IDEAL
TY IN GEORGIA

PROVIDENCE SPRING

Taylor & Macon

The Fickling Masonic Lodge in Butler has unique art deco motifs. Formed in 1852, Taylor County boasts a solar farm with enough energy to power more than 25,000 homes. The town of Ideal touts the local quality of life on a fun water tower in Macon County, which was established in 1837. Also located in Macon County is the Andersonville National Historic Site, where the Andersonville prisoner-of-war camp held Union captives during the Civil War. The monument at Providence Spring memorializes a spring of natural water that came from the ground in August of 1864.

Stewart & Webster

Providence Canyon, the "Little Grand Canyon," is one of the Seven Natural Wonders of Georgia. The canyon, created by erosion from poor 1800s farming practices, offers outdoor activities for the whole family. Established in 1830, Stewart County relies heavily on the forestry industry. The historic Bedingfield Inn in Lumpkin became the first small-town community preservation project in Georgia. In Louvale, "church row" is one of the most unique religious landmarks in Georgia with three churches and an antebellum school building next to each other. Webster County, formed in 1853, has two historic jails side-by-side.

Sumter

Sumter County, established in 1831, is home to Jimmy Carter, 39th president of the United States. The most photographed attraction in the town of Plains is a larger-than-life peanut featuring President Carter's iconic smile. Carter's 1976 campaign headquarters was located in the old Plains train depot. The oldest church in the county is Friendship Baptist Church, built in the mid 1800s. The art deco Rylander Theatre in Americus has a working 1928 Moller Theater Pipe Organ (one of only three in Georgia). Also in Americus is the Windsor Hotel, built in 1892 with castle-like Victorian grandeur.

Dooly & Crisp

Formed in 1821, Dooly County is one of the state's top producers of cotton and peanuts. Stop by the Georgia State Cotton Museum in Vienna to learn about the crop that shaped our state's history. A unique roadside landmark with a strange history is the Titan I, a Cold War era missile that was dismantled and moved to Crisp County in 1968. Crisp, established in 1905, is the self-proclaimed watermelon capital of the world and also hosts the Big Pig Jig, the Southeast's largest and Georgia's oldest BBQ cooking competition. The library in Cordele is the second oldest Carnegie Library in Georgia.

Georgia's Coast

Effingham
Chatham
Bryan
Liberty
McIntosh
Glynn
Pierce
Ware
Brantley
Clinch
Charlton
Camden

Effingham County, created in 1777 as   one of the state's eight original
counties, has a grand Neoclassical style courthouse. The beautifully restored
Mars Theatre in Springfield is a fun venue for films, plays, concerts, and
other community events. The Jerusalem Lutheran Church, built in 1769, is the
fourth oldest building in Georgia and is believed to have the oldest religious
congregation in the state. The Effingham County Methodist Campground is an
open-air structure with overhead fans and wooden pews.

Chatham

Chatham County, founded in 1777, was the fifth county in the state. The Georgia Historical Society in Savannah is one of the oldest historical societies in the United States. W. B. Hodgson Hall was built for the Society in 1876. The Georgia coast has several lighthouses, but the tallest and oldest is on Tybee Island. The First African Baptist Church, organized in 1773, is said to be the first black Baptist congregation in North America. Forsyth Park Fountain is one of Savannah's most well-known icons. Poetter Hall was the original campus building of the Savannah College of Art and Design—a college for art careers.

Liberty County, formed in 1777, was one of the state's
eight original counties. The Midway Congregational Church,
one of the most scenic historic landmarks in Georgia, dates to 1796, and its
historical society is still managed by descendants of the founders. Dorchester
Academy, founded in 1869 as a school for formerly enslaved African
Americans, is on the U.S. Civil Rights Trail. The old Liberty County jail was
built in 1892 and was in use until 1969. Growing all through southeast Georgia
is the Ludwigia maritima (seaside primrose-willow).

Founded in 1777, Glynn County is   home to three beautiful islands —
Jekyll, St. Simons, and Sea Island. On the southern tip of its island, the St.
Simons Island Lighthouse was built in 1810. The Georgia Sea Turtle Center,
located on Jekyll Island, is a functioning hospital and rehabilitation center
for sea turtles and is the only facility of its kind in Georgia. The Old Glynn
Academy is a public high school in Brunswick that was chartered in 1788. The
1840 wooden school building remains part of the campus. The Jekyll Island
Club opened as a beach resort in 1888.

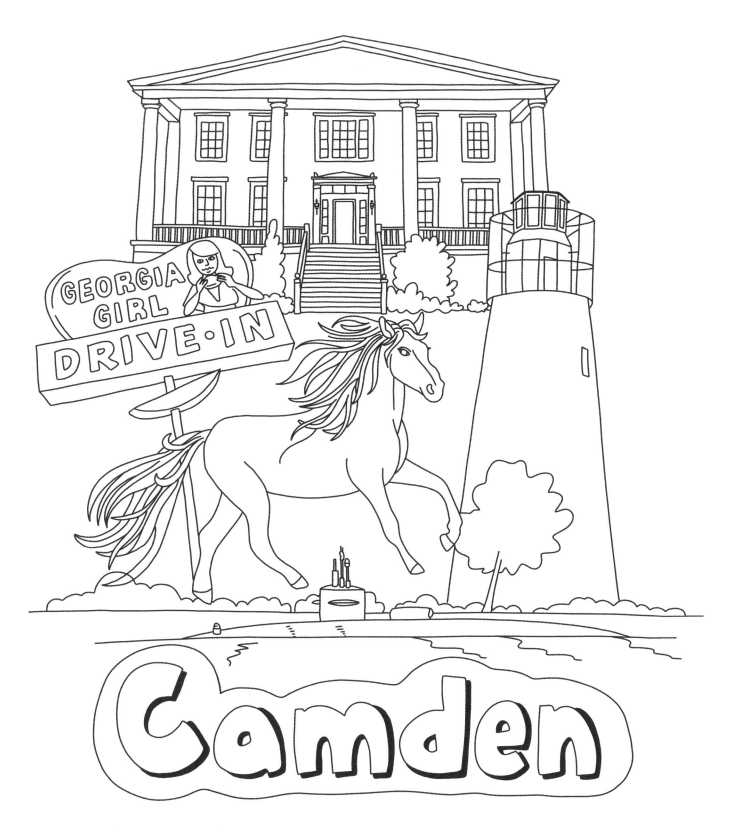

Camden

Created as the state's eighth county in 1777, Camden County is home to the USS Georgia submarine, a guided-missile submarine located at Kings Bay Naval Submarine Base in the town of St. Marys. The Georgia Girl Drive-In in Woodbine has long been closed, but the neon sign remains a popular spot for photographs. Built during the 1830s, Orange Hall is an iconic antebellum home in St. Marys. Little Cumberland Island is home to wild horses roaming free among the marshes and sand dunes. The picturesque Little Cumberland Island Lighthouse, on the north end of the island, is privately owned.

Bryan & McIntosh

McIntosh County, established in 1793, is home to Fort King George, the oldest English fort on Georgia's coast. The Sapelo Island Lighthouse is the nation's second-oldest brick lighthouse. Visitors can take a ferry ride to the island for a tour. Ashantilly, built of tabby in 1820, is a house museum. Tabby is a type of concrete made with ground seashells. Fort McAllister in Bryan County is the best-preserved fortification of the Confederacy. Founded in 1793, Bryan County was the summer home of auto tycoon Henry Ford, who spent much of his personal fortune helping the town of Richmond Hill after the Depression.

Brantley, Pierce & Charlton

Pierce County was established in 1857, and the unique two-story jail was built in 1894. High Bluff Primitive Baptist Church in Brantley County, founded in 1920, was built in 1819 and is still an active congregation. The Gold House Restaurant is a popular spot in the tiny town of Nahunta. The Okefenokee Swamp covers much of Charlton County, created in 1854. The town of Folkston has a very active railroad with 40-60 trains passing daily. Visitors can watch from a custom-built platform in downtown. The Folkston Depot is now a museum dedicated to the town's railroad industry.

Ware County was formed in 1824. The Waycross Journal-Herald building is a unique example of modern architecture in downtown Waycross. The majority of the lower part of Ware County is swampland and the Okefenokee National Wildlife Refuge protects the animals there. The Ritz Theatre in Waycross opened in 1913 and today is used as a community theater. Clinch County, created in 1850, is known as having some of the best honey in the South. The unique taste comes from bees who collect swamp pollen. Antioch Methodist Church is one of the most historic rural churches in south Georgia.

Magnolia
Midlands

Screven

Candler

Bulloch

Montgomery

Treutlen

Bleckley

Laurens

Pulaski

Dodge

Wheeler

Toombs

Tattnall

Evans

Wilcox

Telfair

Jeff Davis

Long

Appling

Wayne

Irwin

Coffee

Bacon

Atkinson

Bulloch & Screven

Screven County, founded in 1793, is home to the first welcome center in Georgia. It is reported to be the oldest roadside welcome center in the U.S. that is still in use. The Seaborn Goodall house near Sylvania was built in 1815. Created in 1796, Bulloch County is home to Nevils Creek Old Line Primitive Baptist Church, which was founded in 1790. It is the oldest church in Bullock County. The Bank of Statesboro is one of the most recognizable landmarks in the city. On the campus of Georgia Southern University is the U.S. National Tick Collection - part of the U.S. National Museum of Natural History.

Established in 1807, Laurens County is home to the town of Dublin, deemed the "Emerald City," and its famed Citizens and Southern Bank Skyscraper, the tallest building between Savannah and Macon. The Dublin Theatre was built in 1934 as a movie theater, and currently it also serves as a performing arts center. The Isoetes georgiana (Georgia quillwort) is known only to grow in five counties of Georgia's Coastal Plains. Its spiky clumps of grass grow in flowing water along the exposed banks of woodland streams.

Coffee County, in south central Georgia, was founded in 1854 and is home to a large section of exposed sandstone called Broxton Rocks. The Broxton Rocks Preserve seeks to conserve the fragile ecosystem. The Silky Morning Glory is an endangered wildflower that grows only around sandstone outcroppings. Coffee's neighbor, Bacon County, was established in 1914 and has one of the most unique banks in Georgia. Pineland Bank, formerly Alma Exchange Bank, has a mid-century modern design. The town of Alma is known as the Blueberry Capital of Georgia and hosts the state's annual blueberry festival.

Atkinson & Irwin

Located in Willacoochee, McCranie's Turpentine Still was built in 1936 and is still largely intact today. Atkinson County was established in 1917, and the county courthouse is a grand structure built in 1920. Salem Church was built in the mid-1800s and also served as a school. Irwin County, formed in 1818, is home to the Georgia Sweet Potato Festival in Ocilla. The festival has been operating on the last Saturday in October every year since 1960. The first documented shape note singing convention in the state was held in Irwin County in 1893.

Created in 1818, Appling County is known for cotton, blueberries and tobacco, three crops that are the mainstay of their rural economy. Canoeing down the Altamaha River, the largest river in Georgia, is a fun adventure for the whole family. The Bank of Surrency was built in 1911 and has been everything from a post office to a bank to a storage facility for sweet potatoes. The Appling County courthouse in Baxley is a grand Neoclassical building constructed of limestone and concrete.

Wayne & Long

Wayne County, founded in 1803, is home to Baptisia arachnifera (hairy rattleweed), an endangered flowering plant that lives among the sandy soil along the coast. The Ludowici Well Pavilion in Long County was constructed in 1907 and supplied drinking water from an artisan well. Created in 1920, Long County is home to the Jones Creek Baptist Church, a congregation that dates back to the early 1800s. The church has memorabilia and other historic artifacts on display. The larger-than-life tin man on Highway 84 between Ludowici and Jesup is a roadside attraction not to be missed.

Founded in 1914, Candler County has turned the 1921 Metter High School building into their Candler County Historical Society Museum. Claxton, in Evans County, is known as the "Fruitcake Capital of the World." The first ecological sanctuary in Georgia was the Charles Harrold Preserve, home to the Georgia Plume—a small tree with fragrant white flowers. Tattnall County, created in 1801, is one of the largest poultry producers in south Georgia. Bland Farms is the largest grower, packer, and shipper of Vidalia onions in the United States. The Alexander Hotel was lovingly restored by the town of Reidsville.

WELCOME TO VIDALIA THE SWEET ONION CITY

Welcome to Santa Claus GEORGIA

"The City That Loves Children"

Georgia 3

Montgomery, Toombs & Treutlen

Established in 1793, Montgomery County is home to a beautiful courthouse in Mount Vernon. The town of Santa Claus, a popular place to get your Christmas Cards postmarked, is located in Toombs County, which was created in 1905. The Southeast Georgia Soap Box Derby in the town of Lyons is the 2nd largest soap box derby in the country. Vidalia onions are the #1 export of this area. Known as the "Sweet Onion City," Vidalia has a fun onion-shaped fountain in the center of town. Founded in 1918, Treutlen County is home to Soperton, often called "The Million Pines City."

Jeff Davis & Telfair

The Orianne Indigo Snake Preserve, set aside to help protect the Indigo Snake, is an undisturbed area of longleaf pines and swampland along the Ocmulgee River. Telfair County, established in 1807, is home to the 1950s Gene Theater in McRae. Today the Gene is awaiting restoration. Another fun landmark in Telfair County is a 35-feet-tall handmade replica of the Statue of Liberty. Jeff Davis County, founded in 1905, has a beautiful courthouse in the county seat of Hazlehurst. The courthouse was built in 1906 and has a unique octagonal pavilion at each of the 4 corners.

Wheeler & Dodge

The Alligator Creek Wildlife Management Area in Wheeler County, which includes more than 3,000 protected acres of wildlife, is home to the gopher tortoise. Sandhill rosemary grows in the sandy soil of Wheeler County, founded in 1912, and smells much like the herb used in cooking. Dodge County, created in 1870, claims the very first Stuckey's roadside store. Their famous pecan log was originally created by Mrs. Ethel Stuckey in the mid-1930s. A unique mausoleum at Orphans Cemetery was erected in 1912 and has a life-size representation of A.G. and Martha Williamson and their nephew.

Bleckley, Pulaski & Wilcox

Cotton, soybeans and peanuts are the mainstays of the economy in Bleckley County. Founded in 1912, Bleckley is home to the Longstreet Methodist Church, organized in 1812. The original church building is still in use. Pulaski County, created in 1808, has a beautiful old Opera House with perfect acoustics. Harness horse racing is a huge pastime of those living in the area, and the county has the only Standardbred Harness training center in Georgia. Founded in 1827, Wilcox County is home to the Ocmulgee Wild Hog Festival which brings attention to the plight of locals who battle the native wild hogs (boars).

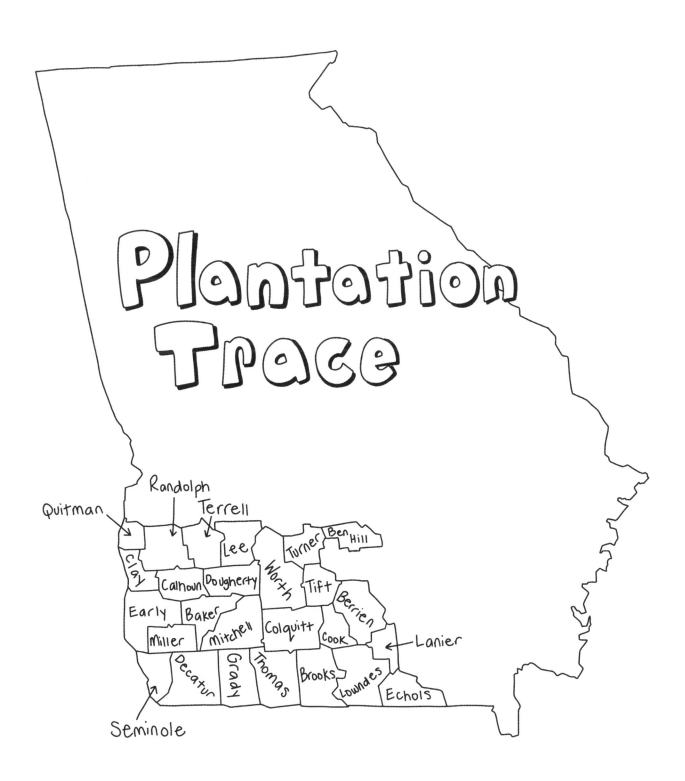

Plantation Trace

Quitman
Randolph
Terrell
Lee
Clay
Calhoun
Dougherty
Worth
Turner
Ben Hill
Tift
Berrien
Early
Baker
Miller
Mitchell
Colquitt
Cook
Lanier
Decatur
Grady
Thomas
Brooks
Lowndes
Echols
Seminole

Lowndes

Built in 1917, West Hall is the oldest building on Valdosta State University's campus. It features Spanish-mission architecture and is the school's center of activity. Lowndes County, founded in 1825, has a Carnegie Library that was designed by local architect Lloyd Green. Today it is home to the Lowndes County Historical Society and Museum. Many wood ducks can be seen at Grand Bay Wildlife Management Area, which includes 18,000 acres of swamp. Families come from all over to enjoy Wild Adventures, a roller coaster theme park with zoo animals, water rides, and a concert venue.

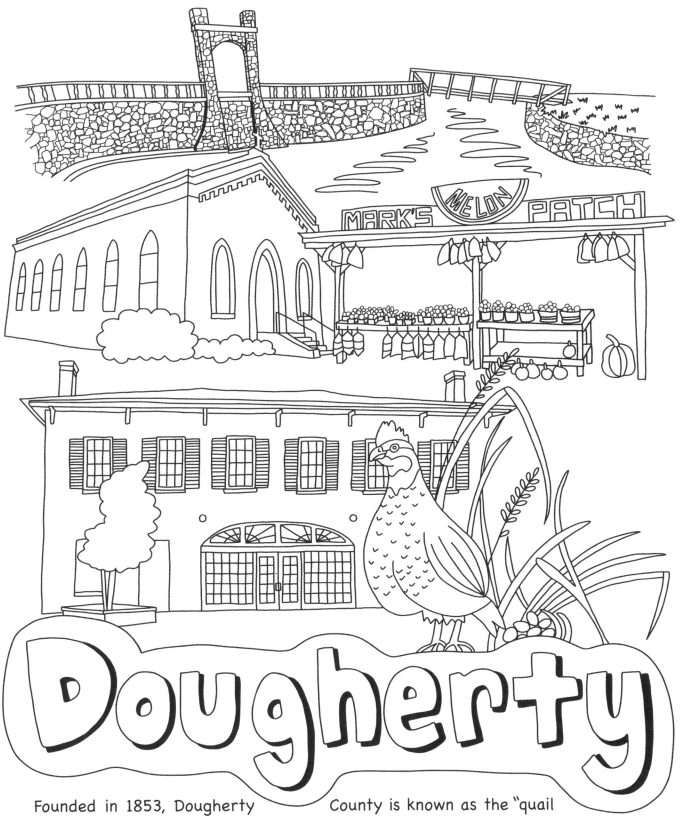

Dougherty

Founded in 1853, Dougherty County is known as the "quail hunting capital of the world." The Bridge House is a historic building designed by famed Horace King. Today it is used as a welcome center. Radium Springs, one of the seven natural wonders of Georgia, is the largest natural spring in the state. The water is 68 degrees year round and contains a tiny amount of radium. The Old St. Teresa Catholic Church in Albany is the oldest active Catholic Church in the state. Mark's Melon Patch is a local roadside market that has seasonal produce and a corn maze in the fall.

Colquitt

Built in the 1960s, the space-age   chapel on the grounds of Norman Park Conference Center, is now part of Shorter University. Established in 1856, Colquitt County is home to the only life-sized elephant tombstone in the world. It marks the grave of Bill Duggan, a circus owner who died in 1950. The old Colquitt County Jail was built in 1915 and is now home to the Chamber of Commerce. Moss Farms Diving in Moultrie is a diving facility which has been the training site for six Olympic teams and has hosted several national diving championships over the years.

Built from 1859 to 1864, the old Brooks County courthouse was one of only two Georgia courthouses built during the Civil War. Brooks County was founded in 1858 and is home to the town of Quitman, known as the Camelia City because of the abundance of the plants grown there. Grooverville, a small community in Brooks County, is home to the historic antebellum Liberty Baptist Church, built in 1858.

The old courthouse in Quitman County, founded 1858, was built through FDR's Public Works Administration. White Oak Pastures General Store in Clay County is located in a 175-year old building and has a wonderful selection for sale. Many endangered plant species live in the area, including Trillium reliquum (Confederate wakerobin), a member of the lily family. The toll-house at Fort Gaines in Clay County, established in 1854, was situated directly above a key bridge over the Chattahoochee. Randolph County, created in 1828, is home to Andrew College, the second college to offer graduate degrees to women.

Terrell County was formed in 1856 and has a very grand courthouse of High Victorian architecture. The old fire station in Dawson was built in 1905 and is still in use today. Lee County, founded in 1825, is home to the Neyami Savannah - an area of boggy grasslands with majestic canopies of cypress trees. Leesburg High School is a historic school building constructed in 1922.

Calhoun, Early & Miller

Calhoun County was established in 1854. Arlington United Methodist Church is the oldest church in Arlington. In Early County, founded in 1818, the Kolomoki Mounds, occupied from 350 to 650 AD, is the oldest Woodland Indian site in the Southeast. You can visit the museum to learn about the Native Americans who lived there. Miller County, established in 1856, is a large producer of cotton, corn, and peanuts. The Mayhaw Festival, which celebrates the tiny tart southern berry, is held every year in Colquitt. Miller County, established in 1856, is home to a huge Native American sculpture by Peter Toth.

Seminole, Decatur & Grady

In Seminole County, founded in 1920, the Olive Theatre originally opened as a silent movie theater. The Old St. John Episcopal Church in Bainbridge was built in 1885 and is the oldest church in continuous use in Decatur County. Shade tobacco barns (for drying tobacco) used to be more common in the South, but very few survive today. Grady County, formed in 1905, has several nicely preserved barns to see. The Pope Store Museum in Cairo was the home of an artist who turned her yard into a folk art masterpiece. The Wolf Creek Trout Lily Preserve is the largest collection of trout lilies everywhere in the world.

Ben Hill, Worth & Turner

Released all over the state for hunting in the 1960s, many Burmese chickens call Fitzgerald home. The Wild Chicken Festival is a fun event for the whole family. Ben Hill County, established in 1906, is home to the Blue and Grey Museum, which strives to tell the story of Union and Confederate soldiers who created the town of Fitzgerald. The Penstemon dissectus (cutleaf beardtongue) is a native plant with small, purple flowers. Turner County, established in 1905, has the unique Crime and Punishment Museum in their historic jail. The smallest library in the U.S. is located in Worth County, created in 1853.

The old store on Ichauway plantation, near the banks of the Ichawaynochaway Creek (yes, that's really the name), is a local landmark. Baker County, founded in 1825, is home to a large forest of longleaf pine trees located within the Jones Research Center, a facility keen on teaching land and water conservation practices. Modeled after Marshall Field's Department Store in Chicago, the Hand Trading Company in Pelham is an unusual site (at 4 stories high) in this rural Georgia setting. Mitchell County, created in 1857, has a beautiful art deco courthouse built in 1936.

The Big Oak is an oak tree located in Thomasville that is estimated to date back as far as 1680. Founded in 1825, Thomas County is home to the historic Boston police department, which was originally built as Boston City Hall in the late 1800s. The B'nai Israel Synagogue, built in 1913, is one of few surviving pre-World War II Orthodox synagogues in the state. A beautiful example of an antebellum plantation house in Thomas County is the Hardy House, which is open for tours. Every spring since 1920, Thomasville has hosted their annual Rose Festival with flower shows, parades, fireworks, concerts, and more.

Berrien, Tift & Cook

Berrien County, founded in 1856, has the original Spirit of the American Doughboy statue to honor those who died during WWI. The beautiful Berrien County courthouse was built in 1898. In Tift County, created in 1905, the beautifully restored Tift Theatre has been delighting movie-goers since the mid-1930s and today it can host a variety of gatherings. The pink Town Terrace Motel has been in business as a hotel, and now apartments, since the 1940s. Cook County, created in 1918, is home to many migrating black and turkey vultures. They roost in trees and soar overhead at Reed Bingha State Park.

The Lanier County Grammar School, built in 1925, is a unique example of early 20th century architecture. Lanier County was formed in 1920 and is home to the Banks Lake National Wildlife Refuge. Banks Lake is mostly shallow black water and has a gorgeous canopy of cypress trees. More than 90% of Echols County is covered with pine forests and most of that is privately owned. Echols County, which was established in 1858, actually has no incorporated towns and is known as the "carrot capital of the South" for its ability to produce millions of pounds of carrots each year.

Index

Laura Murray finds inspiration for her artwork in the people she meets and the region she calls home — going on weekend trips, touring local museums, trying out mom-and-pop restaurants, and driving through small towns. Laura is a designer, illustrator, author, maker of things, coloring book lover, and student of all things beautiful. Her first book, Amazing Alabama, was released in November 2017. Learn more about her work at www.lauramurraycreative.com.